And Quiet Flows the Teesta & Other Poems

Saakal Ulysses Dewan

BlueRose
Publishers
NewDelhi • London

First Published in February 2022

ISBN: 978-93-93388-24-7

BLUEROSE PUBLISHERS

www.bluerosepublishers.com

info@bluerosepublishers.com

+91 8882 898 898

Cover Design:

Muskan Sachdeva

Typographic Design:

Ilma Mirza

Distributed by: BlueRose, Amazon, Flipkart

*Dedicated to The Seekers of Truth,
Goodness and Beauty*

Foreword

Having no claims to any literary achievement so it came as a surprise that a request should come my way to write a foreword. But coming from a former student, the surprise was cushioned a bit. Then again, going through his works a doubt started creeping in 'had I bitten off more than I could chew' because in front of me was a compilation of deep, moving and thought provoking pieces of sublime pleasure. A thought came that I should approach Saakal and tell him that he should approach some personality who was more familiar with the topic at hand and in a way earned himself or herself the honour to pick up the pen. However, another thought swept my mind that this may be the only chance to come my way to some literary fame in that, 'this is the character who wrote the First Foreword,' thus I continue with the Foreword Forwarded.

What first struck me was the way where he 'broadly grouped' his creation. It reminded of the ICSE and ISC text books of yesteryears that I sorely missed. Long time back these text books contained over a hundred poems neatly classified in suitable collections but with the passing of time the numbers dwindled and now we have with us only the few poems prescribed by the syllabi. There is simply no scope for an interested student in meandering along the byways of poem-land to do any loitering and daydreaming. Maybe it is due to environmental concerns where excess use of paper is to be curtailed or maybe it could with the consideration to the purse strings of the parents/guardians but whatever it be the beauty of poetry fails to reach the younger ones. -- This was only the first impression.

Next, some of the topics chosen like Nature, Love and Reflections are what one would term as the usual or traditional stock, not that Saakal has handled them with any less dexterity but it is the other genres that had my curiosity roused and I actually started with last subject 'Corona' first. It is written most remarkably. Thus, with my appetite whetted, just reading through it lasted only one night all read in the reverse order.

Some, Saakal has written in the formal way keeping rhyme and meter in mind but for others he has used the modern approach. This actually made it all the more enjoyable.

Another intriguing commodity Saakal has skillfully used is putting old wine into new bottles. Taking the current situation and a little bit of current affairs he has placed a delectable meal for all of us to savour.

I find it most difficult to single out any one poem or even a group and say that this is the best or even better than the others because every single creation is truly a work of art. Singing parodies of almost anything we sang could have been the spring board in this direction.

I am reminded of a saying of a critic during the days when the Beatles were on the rise. It was flatly stated, "You can either love them or you can hate them but you cannot ignore them." So let it be with Saakal, but I rest assured that like the Beatles he will make a definite mark in the realm of poetry. His compelling approach will surely catch the eyes and hearts of many a lover of poetry which will be appreciated by all.

It is redundant to wish Saakal all the luck or all the best because of the potential inherently in him coupled with his diligent labour, so all I can say is, "Am impatiently waiting for your next masterpieces!"

Date: 10 Dec 21
Dr Pratap Singh Rai, PhD
Director, BSMI School
Place: Darjeeling

Acknowledgements

For my labour of love to come to fruition, I am grateful to my respected teacher Dr. Pratap Singh Rai, PhD, Director of BSMI School, Lebong, Darjeeling, who took the pain, at my very first request, to write a foreword to this anthology with an additional burden of reviewing my work. His guidance even at this stage of life has only justified the fact that education is a lifelong process in which individuals acquire skills and competencies in formal and non-formal learning settings not only in school but also before school and afterwards throughout the entire life-span.

I must also acknowledge my gratitude to the online news portal Darjeeling Chronicles and Darjeeling Times, who earnestly published my articles including my poems enabling me to reach out to larger masses, and in turn inspiring me to publish my own work.

I am grateful to my naval colleagues Mr Tara Prasad Ghimirey and Sanjog Tamang, my college friends Mr Rajesh Pradhan, Mr Amardeep Chhetri, and Mr Satyajay Sunam, my school friends Mr Kushal Yonzone and Mr Mahesh Lama, Manager, Glenburn Tea Garden for providing me necessary support to publish this work of mine.

I also like to keep in my mind all my friends, well wishers who reposed faith in my potential and encouraged me to write.

Author's Note

Poetry, as the oldest and arguably, also the highest form of literature predating the origin of writing itself, has been defined in many ways by the eminent poets down the ages. Through its universal appeal, it has borne the essence of human civilization in the annals of history. Much has been said about it persuasively in seminal works like PB Shelley's 1821 essay A Defence of Poetry, all unanimously eulogizing the most sublime form of human arts. Today, it only warrants me, regardless of my qualification, to touch on the subject that is no less an ocean in so far as the dimension of human creativity is concerned as I have dared to flow as a stream - by publishing my debut anthology **And Quiet Flows the Teesta & Other Poems**.

Frankly speaking, I had bad experience with poetry in my school days as we used to cram the poems and recite before our language teachers by hook or crook, and in the process were unable to appreciate the beauty of poetry. I could not enjoy the music fully that flowed with the verses, and I think, in hindsight, I did injustice to the poets during those days. This saga did not end with school, it only accentuated when we entered our college classes. Then the poem analysis became more technical, almost like mathematics, breaking the stanzas into various components of stressed syllables with their accompanying feet and metrical or rhyming scheme,that appeared almost a puristic exercise to me. Being a student of science, more often than not, I found it boring and tedious in analyzing the stanzas, but I must admit that I was always bemused by the rhymes and imagery of words penned by the poets. I was fascinated by the lure of words which when melded with emotions could evoke surreal feelings. When Wordsworth wandered as a lonely cloud, I felt I was also flying with him in the sky and saw the sprightly dance of golden daffodils tossing their heads along river banks, I could hear a sad nightingale's song in Shelley's poem and often got stuck between two diverged roads of Robert Frost while taking critical decisions of life. Since antiquity, all great poets by virtue of their unique ability to express powerful emotions through eclectic mix of words and portrayal of nature have caught our imagination and made us lose sense of our present while reading their poems. So, I also began to scribble verses after reaching class X and thus my journey into literary world began with a personal diary, but not in my wildest dreams had I thought of publishing my own poetry. My first poem was published in the

North Pointer Magazine of St Joseph's College, Darjeeling, in the year 1998. Then, I was studying in class XI in science stream, and I was elated to find my poem in the college magazine, (the same poem has been included in this anthology titled "Journey") and one poem that merits special mention is "Love at First Sight" because it was more a proposal love letter written during those days (it's another story that the poem failed to produce desired result). Thanks to the advancements made in the communication technology, diary gave way to social media platform like Facebook, where I got to write regularly, and at times sharing my write ups in popular regional online news portals like Darjeeling Chronicles and Darjeeling Times. And it was only after a while I realized that I had written a good number of poems that would numerically qualify to go for publishing coupled by suggestions of my friends and well-wishers to hit the press, that I am writing now. In the process, I must admit sincerely that I digressed from one shade of human emotion to another, gleaning for words to portray it justifiably. As it is said that writer is someone who pays attention to the world, so I also have endeavoured to touch on diverse themes ranging from love to philosophy and hence have categorized my poems under broad themes of **Nature, Love,**

Politics, Reflections, Philosophy, Science and Corona.

Beginning with my love for nature, inspired by the European romantic movement, I have tried to celebrate our connect with nature by praising its beauty through my poems. As a person concerned about environment, I was disturbed by the developments taking place in the river Teesta in the form of hydroelectric dams, an event met with fierce protests by the indigenous Lepcha community of our region who worship the sacred river. So, I wrote a poem on the majestic river inspired by the myth surrounding it, that we had heard since our childhood days and felt it appropriate to give an eponymous title to this anthology of mine with a hope of drawing attention of world to the plight of culturally significant river of our region.

Coming to love poems, although being shy, reticent and almost unromantic guy during my school and college days, followed by military service, even the regimented naval career could not harden me much in terms of romantic feelings, as I could still swoon over Keats' definition of beauty and I have dared to write on the theme of love greatly inspired by the romantic poets. In sync with Robert Frosts' definition of Poetry, I must say, my emotions did find thoughts and words without much difficulty while writing these poems.

Then in true spirit of literature, I have attempted to capture the public emotion churned by the events of the Gorkhaland agitation that resulted in bandh for more than three months in my hometown Darjeeling in 2017. The famous tourist destination also popularly known as the Queen of Hills has been a hotbed of sub-national movement since 1907 where the local people are demanding greater autonomy in the form of separate state within the framework of Indian Constitution. Disillusioned by the failure of politics to meet people's aspiration, I have outpoured my feelings in the Elegy on Comatose Democracy. Also, with profound respect to Alfred Tennyson, I have dared to take poetic liberty to remix and draw a comparison of his famous poem over the failure of leadership of the Gorkhaland agitation of 2017 in the poem The Charge of the Gorkhaland Brigade.

Under the theme of Reflections, my poems are reflective of events occurring in our society that stirred my conscience by incidents like the dastardly Pulwama terror attacks in Feb 2020, chilling deaths of Asifa and Manisha Balmiki. The poems under the theme Reflections are indeed the very reflection of my various moods affected by my observance of life including books and inspirational quotes from social media like Facebook. I have versified my mixed feelings in the poem Au Revoir- On Retirement from Navy on the momentous occasion of my life when I retired from the Indian Navy after completing initial tenure of engagement.

Being a self-proclaimed bibliophile, I've had brushes with various books on science and philosophy, and I was influenced pretty much by the Indian Philosophy particularly the Advaita Vedanta during my college days in St Joseph's College, North Point, Darjeeling, and that enabled me to write poems on the philosophical nature of life.

My scientific curiosity outpoured in the form of verses when India's ambitious second lunar mission Chandrayaan 2 was about to soft land on the other side of moon's face as I sat in front of the television with a pen and paper. I also wanted to celebrate the event commemorating 50 years of human landing on the moon, so I added a couple of lines under theme of science in memory of the pioneer astronauts. Always fascinated by the starry skies during my childhood, the child in me made me to write the A Dream of Star Trekker. And true to poetry's ability to give insight to culture that creates it, having been born on the cusp of analogue and digital world, I have also shared my feeling on the difference that technology has brought in our lives in my poem The Digital Life.

Finally, I have also attempted to share my feelings over the unprecedented situation brought about by the most baffling health crisis in modern times- The Corona Virus pandemic, which literally brought the world to a grinding halt and whose aftershocks we are feeling even today.

This anthology is my first literary work and comprises of poems that I have written over the years spanning from college days to present time and is an epiphany of moods that dominated my mind at the time of writing. For me, And Quiet Flows the Teesta & Other Poems is a living testimony to Wordsworth's view of poetry as the spontaneous overflow of powerful feelings. Lastly, despite not being a student of literature, and hence, lacking the understanding of nuances of language, but being a passionate fan of poems, this anthology is a result of culmination of my humble efforts to do justice to my passion and good wishes of my friends, and hereby I present my labour of love, in all its beauty and frailties.

I hope the readers would appreciate my work.

Saakal Ulysses Dewan
Date: 14 Dec 21
Place: Darjeeling

Contents

POLITICS

REFLECTIONS

PHILOSOPHY

SCIENCE

NATURE

And Quiet Flows the Teesta

Born in the lap of majestic Himalayas,
Begins the odyssey of the mystic Teesta,
Nurtured by mother Lake Tso Lhamu,
Quietly flows the Teesta,

Rumbling down the ravines and gorges,
Sweeping all that come in her way,
With thunder, kinship she forges,
In monsoon, she loves to play,

Slowly, as symbols of human greed,
Dams across her were painfully built,
Her life was robbed at its prime,
How cruel has come the time,

Now she can't disport with her lover Rangeet,
At holy Triveni, where they had promised to meet,
Even the fiery Rangeet is furious no more,
For, he too, has been tamed to outpour,

Mutely watches the mighty Kanchanjunga,
from above,
At times shedding tears in sadness,

For, her children can no longer play their
game of love,
As selfish mortals continue to indulge in madness,

Now, no more Golden Mahseers play,
Under the glistening sun beam,
Nor the lusty trout does stray,
Homeless, as they all have been,

But must she continue her journey,
As promised, with her lover, till eternity,
Their legend shall endure the onslaught of time,
Leaving legacy of true love, sublime,

On the sleepy banks, paddy fields, besides their
hoes,
When a few weary souls revel in their siesta,
Bringing soothing breeze that from mountain
ward flows,
And quiet flows the Teesta....

A Nemophilist's Wish

Far from the madding crowd,
Away from the hustle and bustle of modern life,
I wish to retire to an idyllic world,
Where raw emotions come alive,

Unscathed by onslaught of modern technology,
Where abounds nature's sanctity,
Cosily nestled in mother nature, holy,
In a world blessed with tranquility...

Ode to Monsoon

I see the dark clouds overcast the horizon,
That reminds the arrival of much awaited
monsoon,
Accompanied by the deafening thunder,
Sounding the onset of the wet season,

Bringing much relief to the parched earth,
With the fresh spells of showers,
To the utter delight of a thirsting bird,
Ending the wait of budding flowers,

Inside home, cloistered myself near hearth,
I enjoy the soothing sound of torrents,
That hit my house tin roof and courtyard,
As incessantly outside, it rains,

And as I peek through my window,
I see blithe kids dancing in the rain,
In jolly mood, bereft of sorrow,
Living a beautiful life, with nothing to complain,

Even the lovers seem to rejoice the season,
As fog conspires to bestow them that special
moment,
Bringing the impetuous souls in unison,
Under an umbrella or some tree shade,

For them, pleasures are many of monsoon,
With amorous sight of wet hair and drenched
dress,
That make any earthly lover swoon,
Over the rising crescendo of voluptuousness,

But most happy would be the farmers,
Who earn by the sweat of their brow,
Desperately longing for it like eternal dreamers,
Hoping good harvest of that they nurture and
grow,

But this lovely season would pass soon,
Copiously drenching over the places of dearth,
Blessing some fortunate souls with special boon,
To enjoy the smell of a rain soaked earth,

Ode to One Fine Evening

Far away, in a distant horizon,
I see silvery clouds afloat in stillness,
As if time has stood for a moment,
To savour nature's beauteousness,
Clouds, reflecting the golden ray of dying sun,
Bathing the green fields below,
Hinting the shepherd, the day is done,
And return from the flushing meadow..

I Am A Gust of Wind

I am a gust of wind,
Here now, soon gone,
I leave nothing,
In my brief sojourn,
Sometimes I am a balmy breeze,
Privy to romance of bees and flowers,
That dance around lovely trees,
Merrily after light evening showers
Sometimes I am a fiery tempest,
To the peril of seafarers,
Infamous for sealing many a sailor's fate,
Yet guiding to a new world full of treasures,
I am the Alpha and Omega of life,
I am in and out of everything,
I am one of the elements in five,
My legacy is eternally enduring...

Stopping by the Mirik Lake

In these tranquil waters of placid lake,
I seek that elusive solace,
Hidden behind the world, fake,
Reflecting the visage of divine grace,
Like shadow, sometimes it follows me,
And then vanish suddenly without a trace,
Playing hide and seek with disquietude and
serenity,
Savouring the halcyon earthly days...

Stopping by the Sunset

As the sunset casts its veil over the horizon,
Note of melancholy surrounds me,
Many days have come, many days have gone,
In solitude, silently I struggle to set myself free,

Unknown vibes of this mysterious existence,
Resonate deep inside my soul,
Uncertain is this life, living in pretense,
Lost in the mundane labyrinth, devoid of goal,

With passing of each earthly hour,
Robbed of unforgiving moments, I near to my end,
Joys that overflowed, anguish that turned sour,
Lost their quintessence in nature's blend,

Like a lost pilgrim, wandering only in hope,
This vagabond yearns for his true abode,
In his eternal quest for ever eluding bliss,
Far away from lesser mortals' reach…

Stopping by the Reyang River, Mungpoo

On the craggy banks of Reyang River,
Where the cool morning breezes blow,
I wish to lose myself forever,
And be part of its eternal flow,
Knowing change is the only rule,
And what comes one day has to go,
The cycle of karma will make round full,
The wisdom all that is needed to know...

Walking Down Memory Lane

Sweetly nestled amongst the misty mountains,
Where silvery clouds kiss the verdant hills,
In the lap of nature, that soothes one's beauteous
sense,
Where northerly winds bring wintry chills,
Meanders the road to my home at every bend,
Along the avenue of blossoming white cherries,
Reminding me of my schooldays well spent,
That I trod on gleefully, bereft of worries,
So nostalgic I become but not in vain,
While walking down memory lane,

The Brook's Story

Silently flows the brook,
On the eternal journey, it undertook,
Meandering through beautiful vales,
Older than ancient lores and tales,
So pristine, so clear, the downstream,
Swiftly passing like a fleeting dream,
Through the thick undergrowth and meadows,
Going astray in monsoon, when it overflows,
And when cricket comes out to merry in evening,
It bathes in golden hue that the sunsets bring,
With the lazy cows huddling around on the banks,
Struggling to make way home in much reluctance,
Watching the joyous water swallow in her sprightly
dance,
Skimming over clear stream, perched on nearby
branch,
While other birds are singing on the trees,
In tune with the blowing evening breeze,
Silently flows the brook, telling her own story,
Replete with beautiful chapters of her eternal
journey,
To be joined by rivulets, and mature into a river,
Knowing not to pause but flow forever,

Mountain Calling

The high mountains up there,
Call me up to lay my soul bare,
But I can only behold their grandeur,
Bewitched, in the sightful thoroughfare,

With silvery clouds wafting o'er,
The sun kissed peaks glistens,
On a halcyon day, in a moment to remember,
This solitary soul quietly listens,

To the call of the mountains, wild and free,
That resonates subtly in cosmic harmony,
In tune with the song of mother nature,
Beckoning me to the loveliest of treasure,

Ode to Robin

One redolent wintry morning,
I saw a Robin sitting on a perch,
Happily singing and dancing,
A sweet spectacle of a joyous little bird,

Every morn it drops by, my near,
It hops, chirps and sings,
Bringing message of hope and cheer,
And then happily takes wings,

For it, nature is always the same,
Change seems to be only our trait,
Hence, while it lives in innocence,
We are ungrateful lot who hastily forget,

Alone, even if it is,
It sings and dances in mirth,
Devoid of human frailties,
My folks, let's learn from this sweet little bird,

On Environment

As we head towards the zenith of modernity,
With all advancements made in the name of
science,
Time has come, folks, to ponder with sincerity,
Over the exploitation of Mother Nature,
in utter defiance,

Avarice and wantonness have usurped our mind,
And ruthlessly we continue to exploit
our Mother Earth,
Just to fulfill our greed more than need, has made
us blind,
How ungrateful have we all become,
noblest by birth,

With total disregard for the generations to come,
We hungrily gorge upon our limited natural
wealth,
We scour the earth and dry rivers with aplomb,
We poison the air and produce
ill-effects on health,

Time will come soon when our progeny
will gasp for air,
When they will struggle for life
in man-made ruins,

When they will curse us, for we showed
them no care,
And we are held responsible for all our
wrongdoings,

Folks, it's high time we woke up and saved
our nature,
Before it becomes too late to make any amends,
If ever, we can call ourselves, noblest creature,
It's in the hand of ours where the future of our
children depends,

So let's begin to conserve our resources so rare,
From stopping of water leakages to switching off
unused light,
From non-use of plastics to planting trees
everywhere,
By living a life watchful and morally upright,

Together we can pass onto our future generation,
The legacy of clean nature we inherited from
our past,
So let us live unselfish, without any botheration,
To let our children rejoice beauty of our nature,
so vast,

The Queen of Hills
(Darjeeling)

Silvery clouds gently wafting o'er the vales,
My hometown cuddled up in mother nature's
warm embrace,
Picture serene, straight from fairy tales,
At vanguard stands the mighty Kanchanjunga, in
all her grace,

So picturesque, in her panoramic view,
Mesmerizing every soul to his delight,
Bringing fresh lease of life, anew,
Truly, my hometown is a paradise on Earth...

LOVE

Ode to Damsel

There stood a damsel, so innocent,
In a pensive mood, lost in her own world,
Her eyes unfathomable, her looks decent,
Lay hid in them, her story untold,

Vaguely staring as if in trance,
Weaving her dreams, so dear,
Surreptitiously, I stole her timid glance,
And for a moment, brought two hearts, so near,

So eloquent in her silence, so radiant in her smile,
Glimpse of her would make life worthwhile,
With myriads dreams in her hazel eyes,
Breathes a soul, so beautiful, under these starry
skies,

Behold her beauty! Cast no evil eye,
Let her spread happiness, joy and cheer,
As our earthly life is bound to pass by,
Let her rekindle feelings, chaste and pure,

The Unrequited Love

Were you so beautiful?
That you cast a spell on me for a while,
Pouring special joys into my life, plentiful,
And warmth of your radiant smile,

Ever since that impeccable first sight,
In my dreams I began to see your lovely face,
Words in disarray, feelings disquiet,
I struggled to speak of the nameless grace,

My heart beats began to echo your name,
And wove dreams, thinking of you,
But you stood at uncomfortable distance,
Unaware of the turmoil, my heart was going
through,

Never did you try to understand,
Or you may have had other reasons,
To not requite my love, so unrestrained,
That sought your acquiescence for all seasons,

And slowly in the mist of time,
Began to fade those feelings, sublime,
Life turned over a new leaf, expectedly,
And I moved on, reluctantly,

Alone, silently, wept my dejected soul,
And gazed at the heaven above,
They say that love is immortal,
But such died my unrequited love…

Afterthought

You blew into my life, like a gust of gentle breeze,
And then swiftly vanished according to your
whims,
Leaving a trail of painful memories,
Blowing into smithereens, my unborn dreams,
How could you smile, robbing my sanity,
With scant regard for my sincere feelings,
Enjoying a hollow life of vanity,
In a murky world of shadowy dealings,
So, quietly I retired to my solitary world,
As many beautiful paths in our life,
Could have never been discovered,
Without getting oneself lost, I realize...

Love Me More, Love Me Less,

Love me more, love me less,
But love me, nonetheless,
O'er the hills, in the wilderness,
Make starry skies, our witness,
Of the love, that's so innocent and pure,
That, in the annals of time, shall long endure,
As a living testimony to our unquestionable faith,
Above the cycle of life and death,
It's in the soul and not the superficial face,
Where lies the true beauty and heavenly grace,
So love me more, love me less,
But love me, nonetheless,
What more is left, in this life to express,
Beyond the sweet words and gentle caress,
But to live the moment to its fullest,
And by blessing others be oneself blessed,
For time shall flee soon, leaving no trace,
Of these special moments and beautiful place,
So, love me more, love me less,
But love me, nonetheless,

Disquietude

Uff! So much discomfiture, and anguish,
In the seemingly never ending wait,
Just to glance over your immaculate blush,
Making way into my heart, straight,
So innocent, so unaware you are,
Of all the turmoil inside me,
With every rising tide of passion, near and far,
I drown and die in my emotional sea,
Yet this obstinate heart yearns to rejoice,
The union with my unwary stranger,
Having heard the feeble voice,
That a thing of beauty is a joy forever...

Phantasmagoria

Round and round turning,
She turned into a rosy hue,
Like the pristine dew of morning,
Fallen from the blue,

She peeps with a timid glance,
Ah! A spectacle of sweet innocence,
And makes my soul sing and dance,
That too in a soft cadence,

Her presence I feel,
Like that of a soothing full moon,
Inside the chasm of bosom, still,
Yearning to embrace the soul soon,

But I see her fading with the shadow,
And I can't behold her anymore,
Leaving me in the realm of sorrow,
Goes away forever, someone I adore...

Shall I Fall in Love With Thee Again

Shall I fall in love with Thee again,
To the delight of my unpretentious heart?
And once more savour that bittersweet pain,
That stoically taught me my own life's worth,

Shall I court that feeling of unease?
That takes me on a roller coast ride of emotion,
Within my own world and beyond its reach,
Far into the realm of limitless imagination,

Shall I fall in love with Thee again,
And rekindle the heartburn that till this day lay
cold,
And err beautifully loving Thee in vain,
Or simply retire to my own new found world?

Shall I be greeted by those forget-me-nots and
daisy,
Or I have to walk on the thorns once again?
With shattered dreams behind-just tell me,
Shall I fall in love with Thee again???

Stranger

One more time shall we become strangers,
Said the moon to the dumbfounded morning star,
Stunned remained he to her capricious behavior,
Just it knew then that dawn was not far,

How could our blossoming tryst be so temporal,
Wondered the star bemoaning his destiny,
Only to see her waiting for him as the night fell,
For their love was to outlast eternity...

Angst

When the lady night puts on her cloak of
darkness,
And her silvery darling is about to arrive,
It's in such veiled moment of ethereal stillness,
That the angst of longing for beloved comes
alive,

Love
Over that ever widening distant horizon,
I see the azure sky melt into the emerald sea,
And then quietly I slip into oblivion,
Thinking, is that how our love would be,

Serendipity
Was it an act of divine providence,
Or just an oddity of serendipity?
That to my soul you bore an uncanny semblance,
As if we vibed together from eternity,

Heart

Dear heart, I know one day you will stop to beat for me,
And my eyes will not be there to see,
No longer shall I be able to behold the beauty,
As this life embarks on its final journey,
The sweet memories echoed in those countless beats,
Shall be silenced forever as this soul humbly retreats,
To the primordial abode where I existed before I was born,
Having played my role with fellows I had known,

Inamorata

Almost a blurred reality,
Tinged in my sanity's velvet twilight,
In mutative forms of ephemeral beauty,
I see your faint silhouette,

What should I call you?
When by any name, rose would smell equally
sweeter,
Need I look for any other clue,
That would portray you much better?

I just wish to look deep into your oceanic eyes,
To see the reflection of your innocence,
I beseech Thee, not to forbid me from occasion
like this,
The moment that I have longed for ages,

Let's partake of these precious moments wholly,
Before from our hands they slip away,
Drenched in the drops of eternity,
Thereafter I go mine, and you go your way,

I Love the Way

I love the way your eyes blink,
When you steal away my gaze,
Leaving me speechless, unable to think,
With passion inside my bosom, set ablaze,

I love the way your lips falter,
In your solemn expression,
A spectacle that no force can alter,
So loveable, casting an eternal impression,

Phantasm

She wears darkness,
Like the queen of night,
And vanishes in the wilderness,
With the daybreak light,

Her shadowy moves, I can feel,
An epitome of elegance, in all her grace,
That slowly fades, holding moments still,
As I awaken from my dreamy phase,

Conversation in Silence

If ever you long for tranquil solitude,
And wish to feel the nihility's presence,
Just think of me in certitude,
For, I too, am eloquent in silence,

Then we shall converse in subtle vibes,
Beyond the realm of earthly definition,
Cherishing the true essence of our lives,
We shall revel in the glory of self-realisation,

Strangeness

Nature may bestow upon Thee, the heavenly symmetry,
But Thou may just be a blossom in an unknown wilderness,
For, this soul knows of no exquisite beauty,
Without a little touch of strangeness,

Fantasie

The discordant contours of my untamed
imagination,
Seek to trespass the confines of my limited senses,
Like the ever widening waves of a mighty ocean,
That kiss the shores with profound love, always,

And they transgress into the ethereal realm,
Where reality melts along with child's fantasy,
Borne of thoughts, distilled in a quiet dream,
To make my soul revel in an unearthly ecstasy,

Should I Tell You

Should I tell you that my love is selfish,
And I can't breathe without you,
And that I often err to plunge into your dreamy
eyes,
To the depth of love, fathomed by few,

Should I tell that I remember you in joy and pain,
And deluge my mind with lovely memories,
replete,
Should I tell you that our love shall always
remain,
Like the distant moon, beautiful but incomplete,

Doubt that sun moves along a heavenly line,
Doubt that truth is a lie,
Doubt those zillion stars of night that shine,
But never my love for you till I die,

Love at First Sight

Though strangers are we,
We have our hearts to feel,
The subtle moments of love,
With or against our will,

When I first saw you,
Everything for me became new,
And I lost my life of past,
In my quest to make you first and last,

Since then, my lovely nights have become,
An endless dreary ocean to overcome,
Thinking of you only I sleep,
And wake up in the morning to weep,

For I had seen you in my dream,
Like an angel beyond this realm,
Sweetly smiling in acquiescence,
Making me feel love's presence,

You may not know,
In this world of false-show,
What you mean to me,
How lovely you are to see,

And when I know that,
With moments our life fades away,
I still carry the burden of hope,
That we will be together one day,

Though this may be only a dream,
Or a futile wish to cherish you,
Or the truth may be even greater,
It is so, because I liked you better,

Know that I am of stubborn faith,
That I adore you till my death,
Even if Heaven comes in our way,
I'll not be away from you even for a day,

I have been so emotional,
That my feelings find their way,
Into the unfathomable ocean of poetry,
Drifting away from own life,
I utter your sweet name, night and day,
As I pass through the realm of mystery,

Shall I have to endure the agony,
For whole life without you, my Honey?
To what extent should I wait?
Just to obey the decree of fate...

POLITICS

Elegy on Comatose Democracy

I have a hunch this time too,
That the leaders would succeed to woo,
The gullible and selfish voters again,
And pile up the misery on their unending pain,

For generations have they voted,
And every time they have been cheated,
Robbed of their dreams they nurtured silently,
Had their aspirations die alone but violently,

So accustomed have now become our people,
To the ubiquitous corruption that has made them
feeble,
That no more can they raise their voice,
Nor can they make a proper choice,

In the situation of confused leadership,
When the main issues are at back seat,
This bizarre, painful saga of political exploitation,
Seems to continue despite our frustration,

As we live in a paradox called democracy,
Where citizens are suppressed by their own
elected autocracy,

Only during election, it is assumed to be followed,
Thereafter no interaction is allowed,

As power shifts from people to the elite class,
Who begin to rule living in the house of glass,
So thick-skinned they turn out to become,
That they find problems of poor, cumbersome,

They continue to exploit the weakness of poor,
Keeping them ignorant, half-fed to win next election for sure,
And ironically, the people would vote them again,
Forgetting all their earlier travails and pain,

When they had pleaded for a fair share of governance,
Just to be ignored by the exponents of recalcitrance,
Who continue to devour power like never before,
And are hungry for more and more,

This vicious cycle continues to haunt,
Knowing not that pain only leaves after lesson is learnt,
Still unable to cure people from retrograde amnesia,
Who tend to forget so soon their melancholia,

Is this the idea of democracy?
That had born out of ideals of minds
revolutionary,
When the Bastille was stormed by the oppressed,
Who were offered to eat cake when they didn't
even have bread,

Liberty, equality and fraternity, the battle cry of
French Revolution,
Beautifully adorns the preamble of our great
constitution,
And sadly, today we face only discrimination,
In our society, causing much consternation,

What even if our nation woke up to freedom
many years ago,
We, the poor, the voiceless are always sidelined
from the main show,
The tryst with our destiny is still our dream,
Impossible to be realised with the current team,

The great freedom fighters must be crying in
heaven,
Seeing their holy land in today's condition,
Where the political masters have just exchanged
their skin color,
While the subjects are in perpetual slavery and
stupor,

My heart becomes heavy as I write this elegy,
On the comatose state of our democracy,
But still I have that glimmer of hope,
That the fire of Renaissance, this generation will
stoke,
And lit up ideologically dark sky with many a star,
That the majoritarian politics had denied the
minority so far...

The Lotus-Eater Gorkhas of Hills

Stupefied by the worldly fame,
On being labeled as the greatest martial race,
Sadly today struggles to assert its name,
And, in the crowds, seeks to recognise its face,

Tagged with a name of mercenary,
So faithfully you served your masters,
Brought resounding victories in battlefields many,
Equanimous in both triumphs and disasters,

Unhesitatingly you crossed the seven seas,
Just at the Crown's clarion call,
And blew the trumpet of victories,
That sounded many empires' downfall

You fought for freedom of Mother India,
Serving in the ranks and files of INA,
Joined the mass struggle, under Gandhi's idea,
On the land, that today, doubts your DNA,

Where is the credulity and valor?
That your masters had once seen in your face,
In your prime, you look so senile, robbed of
power,
Pining for redemption, fallen from the grace,

Your feeble voice is now lost,
In the din of political pandemonium,
The sacrifices of your brave ancestors have come
to naught,
As self betrayal, avarice, all have brought you into
odium,

You traded your dream and aspiration,
With the new political masters of Kolkata and
Delhi,
Gratifying yourselves, unmindful of collective
destination,
Made conspicuous by your bulging belly,

Now, you have to stop playing self victim,
You have to rise like Phoenix from ashes,
And restore the pride and self esteem,
That have been lost in history's pages,

So, awake, arise from deep slumber,
Oh valiant Gorkhas, stop not till your goal is
reached,
Walk along the path of virtue, worthy to
remember,
Pause not till every soul is freed....

On 17 Jun 2017 Firing (Singamari, Darjeeling)

Eerie silence slowly overtook,
Once vibrant place made a somber look,
And turned into a ghostly town,
Walls screaming, air conspiring,
Few lionhearts treading the unfair warzone,
Every head wondered what was the crime,
Of those innocent souls who met cruel fate,
Who loved their motherland more than anything
else,
The supreme sacrifice they had just made,
The holy land was made purer by their blood,
Spilled by the blind adversary who never had a
second thought,
That this fight was against injustice and nothing
else,
That love for our motherland in our hearts forever
dwells,
Cometh the sunshine, cometh the rain,
Oh, brave souls! Your sacrifice shall never go in
vain,
Generations to come shall remember you,
Tearfully as we bid you adieu…

The Charge of Gorkhaland Brigade

(This poem is remixed version of The Charge of the Light Brigade by Lord Tennyson, the poet here compares the Gorkhaland agitation of 2017 with the fateful mission of the Light Brigade)

Half a league, half a league,
Half a league onward,
All in the fight for self-dignity,
Rode the souls innocent,
"Give me your faith!
I will give your land" he said,
In the struggle for identity,
Many innocent souls bled,
"Forward, the sons of brave,
Was there a man dismayed?"
Not though the soldier knew,
Someone had blundered,
Theirs not to make reply,
Theirs not to reason why,
Theirs but to do and die,
In the struggle for identity,
Was martyred a few souls innocent,
Unaudited works to right of them,
State's diplomacy to left of them,
Strategies out run and boomeranged,

Stormed at with shot and shell,
Boldly they fought and well,
Into the jaws of death,
Into the mouth of hell,
Walked the souls innocent,
Unsheathed all their khukris bare,
Flashed as they turned in air,
Catapulting stone here and there.
Charging the police, with hands bare,
Whole the hills wondered,
Plunged in the tear gas smoke,
Right through the line they broke,
Stormed at with shot and shell,
While one by one heroes fell,
They that had fought so well,
Came through the jaws of death,
Back from the mouth of hell,
All that was left of them,
Left of souls innocent,
When can their glory fade?
O the brave challenge they made,
All the world wondered,
Honor the supreme sacrifice they made,
Honor the Gorkhaland Brigade,
The noble souls innocent…

REFLECTIONS

Reflections

To every beginning,
There is an end,
No matter how much I pray,
Or how much I pretend,
So, how does it matter,
If I rejoice or cry,
World's gonna continue to exist,
Even after I die,
Sun will continue to rise with its golden glow,
So will moon shine in the silvery night,
And the placid brooks will continue to flow,
Quietly under the celestial starry light,
My emotions may weigh on me,
Like the insurmountable mountain,
But soon they shall flee,
With the softly dying pain,
So, why should I seek permanence?
In this ephemeral world of dream,
When I am living a life in pretense,
Flowing in a consciousness stream...

Inner Voice

From the deep recess of my bosom,
Springest a voice, feeble but clear,
And says our future to be worrisome,
With clairvoyance of a seer,

Enough! It says, world has rotten,
It's time to purge the unholy,
Virtue; mankind has forgotten,
How great has been our folly...

A Wish of a Solitary Soul

If I should die,
Think only this of me,
There was a soul with thoughts high,
Who yearned to be free,
Free from the prejudices,
And trivialities of this mundane world,
Free from the vices,
That make up for human fault,
And a wish to soar into the limitless sky of
freedom,
Above the clouds of parochial thought,
To enjoy the bliss of stardom,
That small mind could have never brought,

Choices

To be or not to be, is the question,
And in it, lies the path of our life's destination,
We were born not out of our choice,
But we live now, and have our own voice,
We make our mar our future, it's up to our will,
Our action decides our fate regardless of what we feel,
It's always a decisive moment to say either yes or no,
For, the repercussions are far beyond than what we know,
At every perilous bend of our life's journey,
And at the bewildering crossroads that we meet many,
We shall meet the devil of dilemma, upright,
From whom we cannot neither flee nor hide,
Waiting eagerly to feed on our choices,
On bad ones it laments, on good ones it rejoices,
And the life that we naively live now,
Is always caught in the predicament of choices row,
You are only one decision away from a totally different life, someone said,
For everything in our life is a reflection of choices that we have made...

Wish

Sometimes I wish to write a story,
A story of a soul imbued in an air of melancholy,
For whom the world is just an illusion,
That condemns everything into oblivion,

Sometimes I wish to pen a song,
A song that would right every wrong,
And lift the gloomy spirit up high,
To savour the resplendence of sunny sky,

Sometimes I wish to scribble a poetry,
Versifying my feelings about heavenly beauty,
That embraces our little world in fullest measure,
And rejoice in small deeds of kindness with
pleasure,

In my own small world of childish fantasy,
I want to live and die happily,
Away from the beguilement of madding world,
Alone, reflecting upon my solemn, pure thought,

Ode to Happiness

Oh happiness! Tell me, where didn't I seek thee?
In the realms of senses and beyond,
In every step of life's arduous journey,
In every struggle to free from earthly bond,

Oh happiness! How I sought thee, high and low,
Drifting in the ocean of samsara, alone,
Chasing like the ever following shadow,
Clinging to hope until the voyage is done,

Unbeknownst to the riches and worldly fame,
Thou chose to stay in a pure mind,
Residing in the heart of soul, tame,
In simplicity, is where, one could find,

Thou promised to appear,
Only when I let my expectations to disappear,
And from outside thou never flow,
Thou were just my mindset, finally I came to
know...

Ode to Greatness

Thou, never a foster child of fate,
That lesser mortals believe to be,
Thou, favour only those, blest,
With character and vision to foresee,

Thou, craved by kings and men alike,
Thy gentle touch, their utter delight,
Thou, seek to challenge their limit,
A seldom guest to the timid,

Thou, borne out of blood, sweat, toil and tear,
Inconceivable to those who know fear,
Thou, bless the gritty and the industrious,
With the crown of glory and history, illustrious,

Neither by the decree of fate,
Nor in the alignment of stars,
If tryst with Thee be ever made,
It be in the shape of battle scars,

Lives of all extraordinary men,
Remind us of the important lesson,
That no one ever achieved greatness,
Without a little touch of madness...

Burdened Hope

When the hope becomes a burden,
Imagine the stretch of tribulation,
That borders the patience of a crestfallen,
Making mockery of his dream and ambition,

No longer, the sunrise would be the same,
Its golden rays would no longer caress,
No star would like to share the blame,
Leaving the moon alone in darkness,

The whole world comes crumbling down,
And dreams scatter amongst the emotional
debris,
Fate itself would upon him, frown,
When tide turns against his favour, miserably,

Shunned by his own aspirations,
Forsaken by his own expectations
Really his life treads on the path of doom,
When the only hope becomes a burden....

Ode to Dejection

In a deep slumber, unable to open my eye,
Into the abyss of nightmare, I fell,
Caught behind everyone, I,
Surreptitiously inched towards a living hell,

Beacon of hope, began to fade,
The charm of success lured me no more,
Alone, through the sea of life I wade,
Drifting listlessly, with no sight of shore,

Clinging onto the hope, fast fading,
Pulled down by evil force,
This lost soul moved on uncomplaining,
Hoping things to turn better from worse,

In darkness, I began to find solace,
And abundance in solitude,
Like the primeval couple, fallen from grace,
In their quest for beatitude,

Beneath the pall of gloom,
A faint ray of hope emerges,
Defying the message of doom,
A renewed spirit arises,

With whatever is left in this broken soul,
Catching the glimpse of beautiful life,
I moved on sluggishly towards my goal,
To emerge triumphant in this mortal strife,

Crossing the Rubicon

There were umpteen choices before me,
One, I had to make, for everyone to see,
And I chose it knowing not why,
Whose repercussions would haunt me till I die,

So with my choice I began to live,
I learned to forget and forgive,
I ventured into new territories,
Burying my past beneath memories,

Breaking the stereotypes, making my own rule,
Embarking on a journey, adventureful,
I challenged the insurmountable,
And faced situations, lamentable,

Standing on the cusp of fleeting time, I reflect,
Unable to undo the past act,
Now, I have reached the point of no return,
Of life, I have crossed the Rubicon....

Confession of an Obsessive Empath

Yes, I am an empath,
And I care for others,
I identify myself with them,
And their problems, to me bothers,

Yes, I am an empath,
Others' suffering is also mine,
I like to reach out to their feelings' depth,
And rise with them when their mood is fine,

Yes, I am an empath,
I can't see the tears of sorrow,
Why can't there be peace? I ask,
And pray to find smiles, tomorrow,

Yes, I am an empath,
Fully aware of my sense and sensibilities,
Bringing smiles in a forlorn face,
Finding life's meaning in these responsibilities...

I put myself into their shoes,
To know how's it to feel the fate's wrath,
And lend my hand to rid their blues,
Just because I am an empath,

Obstinacy

Knowing that this moment is going to pass,
And with it that I hold so dear,
Knowing that this life is just an eye wash,
Whose meaning, only after death, becomes clear,

Yet I cling on those fleeting moments of joy,
That comforts me, however ephemeral,
Defying the will of that create and destroy,
In the grand scheme of Time, the Great
Leveler...

The Bliss of Solitude

Away from chaos, in absolute stillness,
Is where greatest ideas are born,
In the abysmal depth of unspoken silence,
Is where nubile dreams are woven,

Unscathed, undefiled, in its all purity,
The noble thoughts brim over the beatitude,
Romancing with innocence and creativity,
Savouring the bliss of solitude...

Au revoir- On Retirement from Navy

'it was just an ordinary day,
Adieu, when to my first career,I had to say,
Still it seems to me like yesterday,
When we all together had jumped into the fray,

Of exploring the ocean of opportunities,
Amidst the voyage laden with difficulties,
When we reached INS Chilka's hallowed portals,
A new world beckoned us, surely not for lesser
mortals,

Instilled on us, by the GIs was discipline high,
That was to stand in good stead, even when we
were to die,
Hours were split, for gardening to cleanship,
Along with honing skills of seamanship,

One for all, all for one,
That way training went on,
Mistake by one brought wrath to all,
Reminding us, every time we are on duty's call,

We gave our blood, toils, sweat and tears,
Under the watchful martinets many,
Just to become men in white, sans fear,
To ride the waves as sentinels of sea,

Then the green horns set to build the bridges of
friendship across the sea,
Overcoming sea sickness and nostalgia,
Away from homeland and endearing family,
With lingering problems many,

Now I shall miss the smell of mild steel,
That scorching heat of engine room testing our
will,
Those irritating pipes, dictating our lives,
From colours to sunset, that every seafarer
describes,

From morning PT to battle station,
We had all but home port as our destination,
Sailing Friday and entering harbor on Monday,
Countless sacrifice we made of dear Sunday,

When asked for a break post long sailing,
Accused were we of weak spirit, always wailing,
Now, I stand on the cusp of time,
A watershed moment of my life,

As I retrospect a life of mixed feelings,
Vignettes of past, flashes back, torn in strife,
Now, with new challenges,
a new world beckons me,
Young is the spirit still, of this man of sea,

Ready to embark upon a new journey,
To explore the unchartered territory,
For to discover a new world and more,
We should have the courage to lose sight of our
shore…

Life at Sea

Alone, alone, and all alone,
Alone in a wide, wide sea,
My eyes stretch the horizon,
As far as they can see,

In the midst of tumultuous waves
Quartered inside a rocking boat,
From port to port, homeward my soul craves,
Honing skills to fight and to float,

Alone, alone, and all alone,
Alone in a wide, wide sea,
Closed up on duty till task is done,
For eternal vigilance is the price of liberty,

Steely nerves, hawkish vigil,
An embodiment of courage and integrity,
Flag bearers of a proud legacy,
Sums up a mariner's story, if there be any...

The Power of Small

Always care for small things,
For they are the source of all great beings,
Like stream, beginning of everything is small,
In a seed was once, a tree that now stands tall,

A journey of thousand miles begins with a single
step,
In small efforts lies the virtue of adept,
One small hole can sink a mighty ship,
And jeopardize the most adventurous trip,

A battle is lost for want of a nail,
And history is made to script a different tale,
Always care the things that are small,
Over a loaf of bread mighty empires had to fall,

Small is also beautiful, you ask me why,
Just see those little gems above in a cloudless
night sky,
Nature rejoices in the beauty of small,
Else why shines child's smile above all,

It's not in the indulgence of luxury,
Where lies the secret to end misery,
But in little deeds of love and kindness,
That hold the panacea to dispel our sadness,

Challenge

So what if, before me,
Lie mountains of formidable challenges,
And impossible seem the climb uphill,
Stretching to the limit, my raw sinews,

My indomitable spirit shall cling on,
To the unshakeable rock solid faith,
That implore me to carry on,
So long in me, remains my breath,

For, I shall be all eyes to the enchanting view,
That only the summiteers can boast of,
Where earth meets heaven, across the clouds,
few,
A moment of glory to the soul, spirited and tough,

Whether it be scaling the lofty height,
Or finding pearls on the deep ocean floor,
The key is not giving up the fight,
And in it lies the man's finest hour,

So, why not chose a life of a valiant,
Instead of life so unworthy and insipid,
For success comes to those who dare and act,
It seldom goes to the timid...

Monument

Sometimes I wish to build a monument of
memories,
Whose walls would be painted with my past
stories,
Of those beautiful days of bygone years,
Dotted with fun filled chapters that bring me tears,
And whose spires would rise as high as my
dreams,
In whose silent corridors would whisper all
beautiful things,
A monument, that would forever be a part of
eternity,
Bearing my signature, as an immortal testimony,
Lending me my share of contentment,
As we all depart when the world is done,
Knowing that there lies my monument,
Where I continue to live long after I am gone...

So Laugh a Little, Smile Awhile

So laugh a little, smile awhile,
Before this wonderful journey ends up on a pile,
We never know when will be our last show,
And who will be the first one to go,
Life is too short to nurse grudges,
And too long to keep false promises,
So why not live and let live,
With a heart that knows not to take but give,
For our true riches are our unremembered act of
generosity,
Bringing smiles in the faces wrinkled by adversity,
Away from the worldly glare and expectations,
In the true spirit of a good Samaritan,
What's there so nagging that robs our inner
peace,
When the life is bound to fall into time's abyss,
Sooner or later, we shall wake up from this
fleeting dream,
Letting go of all that we held dear, down
consciousness stream
From dust we sprang,
To dust we shall return,
The immortal truth we all sang,
Shall prevail over everyone,
So laugh a little, smile awhile,
Before this wonderful journey ends up on a pile...

Perspective

Strange are the responses of life,
Mixed are always our feelings,
Hell is here, so is paradise,
All depending on our dealings,

Some shut themselves within,
While some dance out in the rain,
Some wear out complaining,
While some find joy even in pain,

Triumph

Through the vast stretches of treacherous ocean,
The sail sets on its arduous odyssey,
Assailed by mighty waves in motion,
It cruises through the bosom of perilous sea,

In the march towards its coveted destiny,
Tempestuous gale shakes the boat,
But the captain persists crossing hurdles many,
With spirit high and hope soared,

Finally, he arrives at his home port,
After the gruesome battle is won,
To be crowned in the royal court,
When the fateful adventure is done,

Patience

Some come early, some come late,
In compliance with nature's grand order,
Much is achieved by him who can wait,
Unperturbed in life's rough weather...

Voyage

Oh God! Your sea is too big,
And my boat is too small,
I have so many promises to keep,
And so short life to fulfill them all,

My destiny is distant miles away,
Beyond the limit of observable horizon,
I need to sail through waters of joy and dismay,
And succeed during this earthly sojourn...

Victory

What if this lonely soul is down with battle bruised
scars,
Remember, little darkness is needed to see even
the brightest of stars,
Not only he, who comes first,
Or is strong, is necessarily a winner,
But the one whose fight is just,
Tastes the victory equally sweeter...

Struggle

In a moment so desolate and forlorn,
Accentuated by the cruel distance of time and
space,
I continued to take care of a life, strife torn,
Hoping to find that much sought after solace,

When the clouds of gloom would clear from my
sky,
And the sun of positivity shine again,
Spreading the radiance of joy, low and high,
Reflecting my struggles that did not go in vain,

Dejected, often I would ask myself, why?
Just then I would gaze at the distant dying sun,
To only realize that we all are under the same
blue sky,
And yet don't have the same horizon,

Individuality

In a world so obsessed with joining the
mainstream,
I wish to flow as a lone tributary,
And quietly live my own dream,
Cherishing the essence of my individuality,

Change

How painful must have been the change,
While losing one's fragment of existence,
But suddenly, the larva in its last try,
Is metamorphosised into a beautiful butterfly,

The flowers that blossom in spring,
Are no more to be seen in the fall,
Must we heed the changes that seasons bring,
Subject of time we are after all,

Prejudice

What if the edifice of my stubborn belief,
Were built upon prejudices instead of facts,
And I were to witness my character perish,
In indulgence of those unholy acts,

Memory

I have been wearing your memories all along,
Now the vagaries of time seem to blemish them,
Your sweet voice that once echoed a beautiful
song,
Is now lost in the worldly pandemonium,
Oh solitude, where is the innocence that once
adorned your face?
In the rustling winds, I seek going place to
place…

Sojourn

Knowing that I shall pass,
But once, this beautiful place,
Why do I pine for moments to last?
When even the blazing sun goes down with
grace,
What is this life all about,
A quaint medley of pleasure and pain?
That connives with me to live in doubt,
Knowing that I shall not pass here again…

Faith

What if you are going through the worst,
Or have a feeling that life sucks,
Never abandon the faith in your heart,
For it's only the broken instrument that works,

Resilience

When you change your direction,
Don't expect the same wind to greet you,
Just brace yourself for every situation,
For in every turn, life demands you to
say,"Adieu,"

Remember, it's only in the deepest pain,
That we realize the profoundest wisdom,
And it's the darkest hour again,
That precedes the brightest dawn,

Mist

Oh! How I wish to lose myself, often,
Into the nebulous mist of time,
And catch the glimpses of immortality,
Trespassing the last frontier of my wildest
imagination,
Into the mist that engulfs all,
That is under and above the blazing sun,
Holding the secrets many, hidden,
And destiny of earthly mortals...

Dream

Sometimes, too big a dream is a burden,
To a small head full of imagination,
Yet in dreams we live and breathe,
And feel the presence of our sorest need,

Endeavour

Destiny is about of our choice no matter how abstruse,
The fights we don't fight are the ones we chose to lose,
So, arise, awake and conquer before you die,
Make your every moment count and worthwhile,
When life gives you a hundred reasons to cry,
Give life a thousand reasons to smile,
Success comes only to those who dare and act,
It seldom goes to the timid,
We need to live by this undeniable fact,
And explore the opportunities of life, infinite,

Trust

Trust not the world for it never payeth that it
promiseth,
How long will people remember after you are
dead?
Seize the moment, live it to the fullest, it's the only
hour,
Rejoice, be merry, nothing will last forever,

Ephemerality

You can never see the same me twice,
As with time my old self dies,
In a constant flux is our life,
So what is there so nagging for us to oblige?

Life

Life- a momentary occasion to cherish,
From deep inside inner voice screams,
To die with fond memories,
And not with unfulfilled dreams,

Signature

On the canvas of my imagination,
Quietly, I paint my feelings, alone,
Feelings that overflow the limitation,
Imposed by the stereotyped tradition,

With vivid colors of my wild fantasy,
Vying to lend that surreal symmetry,
To a masterpiece in the exotic gallery,
My very signature in the pages of eternity,

Paradox

How strange! Our sweetest songs tell our saddest
thoughts,
In abysmal ignorance lies our profound wisdom,
And the essence of music lies not in varying notes,
But in the imperceptible silence between them,

How incredible is our modern society,
That it cannot drink the truth pure,
It has to be denatured with small dose of falsity,
Before it can be served to us impure,

The masquerading truth that appears in many a
form,
In hope, in expectation, in dreams and in feeble
wish,
Perfectly poised to perpetuate the wisdom,
To reign in a world where ignorance is bliss,

Ulysses

In true spirit of the Greek legend,
Thou left to conquer the ever expanding horizon,
Across the deep Cosmos, beyond the heaven,
Hail the Ulysses, the conqueror of mighty Sun...

Shadow

Nature, to us, has already shown,
The Truth, all we need to know,
It's only when sun goes down,
That small men cast long shadow...

Journey

In the mist of time,
A man continues his journey,
Accompanied by thoughts many,
Leading him towards unknown destiny,

For whole life he travels
Not taking a sigh of relief,
Incessant in his pursuit,
Attached firmly to his belief,

He crosses the bewildering world,
Full of illusion and mystery,
Never does he pause, for,
He claims to make history,

Defying the allure of this world,
Towards the Divine he marches on,
For it is his very own destiny,
Cherished by none,

Now he achieves the Enlightenment,
And the face of plurality fades away,
Finally he is blessed with the attainment,
On completion of his spiritual journey,

The Seed of Resilience

They tried to bury me,
Not knowing I was a seed,
Now I shall rise slowly,
And re-establish my own creed,
Dropped in the dirt,
Confined in the darkness,
Still I shall rise upward,
Regardless of reverses,
Never shall I cower down,
Before the face of circumstances,
I shall make it source of inspiration,
No matter how daunting the challenges,
Greater the duress on me,
Brighter shall I shine,
Like the unpolished ruby,
Extracted from mine,
I shall walk through the fire,
And come out as gold,
Unfazed by situation, dire,
With adventures untold,

Ode to Hermes

I beseech Thee! Oh the swift one
More subtle than ether
Swifter than our thought
Thou, on decree of majestic Zeus
Trod the sublime Mt Olympus
Bearing oracle of both immortals and mortals
Thou mutate faster than time
And render us inquietude
I beseech Thee! Not to carry my mind in thy wings,
wings,

Ode to Poverty

Just because I am smiling doesn't mean the whole
world is happy,
Just because I have no problems doesn't mean
others are tension free,
There are people fighting for their survival,
With an eternal hope for their fortune's revival,
Struggling to keep the wolves from the door,
everyday,
They toil, they sweat and they pray,
Fighting against the harsh circumstances,
That the cruel twist of fate has made their
nemesis,

Imposing unfair conditions on them,
With only birth being left to blame,
Was the mother so guilty to breed a poor son?
Or the sycophantic society is the real reason?
For, sun rises for everyone, rich and poor alike,
And so does nightingale sing her song of plight,

How did discrimination creep in our natural
order?
How our pure state of nature got sullied, is a
point to bother,
Just because they are poor doesn't mean they
have no voice,

They are just made to accept everything, as they
have no choice,

Our life's mission should be to reach out to every
such unfortunate soul,
For we could have been one of them, had the
fate not played its present role,
They shiver at biting cold, they get drenched in
monsoon spells,
They do seek reprieve from searing summer heat,
when their shelter fails,
Their pain is same as ours, it is a universal
language,
Just because they don't speak doesn't mean they
don't have a message,

Dear folks, they do speak but with a faint, feeble
voice,
That gets lost in the din of modern consumerist
society's noise,
So, it's our noble duty to love our underprivileged
siblings,
And always harbour their sufferings in our
feelings,
Help ever and hurt never, should be our
ambition,
In order to claim ourselves as God's finest
creation...

A Tribute to Pulwama Martyrs (14 Feb 2019)

A dastardly attack by the loathful cowards,
Shook the conscience of a peace loving nation,
Supreme sacrifice made by our bravehearts,
Shall always be remembered by generations,

On donning the uniform, the very first day,
You had vowed to protect this great country,
After all, no easy task is it to say,
To be in the line of duty,

Now you're the fallen heroes,
Amongst your dear comrades,
With them, you will mingle no more,
Nor accompany them during routine raids,

Your laughter they will miss,
About girlfriends, no more will they tease,
At home, your absence will be terribly felt,
For in their hearts, whole life you have dwelt,

Your sacrifice shall not go in vain,
Your brothers - in-arms will strike again,
Justice shall be done to you,
As the nation tearfully bid you adieu...

Death of Innocence-
Asifa Bano

An act of unspeakable brutality,
Crushed the tiny soul innocent,
Painfully, we witness a dying humanity,
Ashamed are we, God's creation noblest,
What was her crime, what was her fault?
Was it conspiracy of time itself she knew not?
Conscience shaken, souls scarred with her
absence,
Tearfully, we grieve on the death of innocence,

Justice to Manisha Balmiki

Oh Baba Saheb! See what freedom have we got,
Today we hang our heads in shame,
There has been no respite in spillage of blood,
As hate crimes continue in Dalit's name,

Hardly had we forgotten our Nirbhaya
Whose death had shaken the conscience of
nation,
We witness the ghastly crime again today,
A malady of society mired in caste subjugation,

When shall our girls breathe air of freedom?
When can our womankind feel secure?
When can they break the traditional male
bastion?
How long have they to endure?

Silently weeps many an innocent soul,
As countless stories go unheard across our
nation,
Time has come to vigorously pursue your goal,
Paving the way for caste annihilation,

Ode to the Year Gone By
(2015)

Caught unawares, again am I,
By the subtle thief called time,
And now, one more year has gone by,
Insidiously robbing my life in its prime,

Once again, I am compelled to retrospect,
The moments, so far, that had laid bare,
And then realize with little guilt,
Just to find it another empty year,

Slowly my life is dying,
Unbeknownst to my present mind,
Yet wishes and hope keep on flying,
Like Cupid struck lovers, blind,

Days passed in tune with the season,
Under the great revolving sun,
Mute I contemplate alone,
For the world will pass into oblivion,

Adieu 2019

So, here comes the time again,
When we look back at the year gone by,
In slight unease and little pain,
For, it's not a year, but a decade that's about to
die,

And with it, many a sweet memory,
Shall be buried beside the bitter experiences,
But both scripting life's beautiful story,
Of struggles, and hits and misses,

Reminding us, nothing in life is forever,
But our little deeds of kindness,
Done in the needed hour,
Like a lamp in the darkness,

Now, Mother Earth has gone full circle,
And the sun is the supreme witness,
We can, but only tearfully bid farewell ,
To the past moments that we cherish,

New challenges will confront us,
From the new dawn of morrow,
With a smile shall we face them, thus,
With equanimity, in joy and sorrow...

Adieu 2020

So, the time has come finally for the parting shot,
To bid adieu the year that was so weird,
Hardly had we stepped into the new year,
When the monstrous Corona spread global fear,
Our humanity was brought to a grinding halt,
Not knowing whose really was the fault,

And then began the tales of unprecedented woes,
With lockdown, forcing widespread job losses,
Reverse migration affected every family,
As their sole bread winners had to return forcibly,

Many had just begun to live their new dreams,
Cut short by the agonising screams,
The screams of marginalised daily wage earners,
And the workers in unorganised sectors,
And to compound their unending miseries,
Even welcome was not accorded by their families,

In the fear of spread of the invisible contagion,
Many a hapless migrants faced social
discrimination,
The dust has not yet settled down,
And the challenge ahead us is still unknown,

PHILOSOPHY

The Metaphysical Me

As I gaze at the vast expanse of Cosmos,
Creepy loneliness slowly surrounds me,
And the daunting enormity of space makes me
realize,
How small is our human family,

So long I flow in this stream of consciousness,
Myriads of thoughts rack my naive mind,
Wandering in the temporal world, seeking
purpose of existence,
And then I die in my pursuit, ignorant and blind,

From dust I springest,
To dust I shalt returnest,
I am part of this universe,
I made up of the celestial star dust,

My atoms will reconfigure into new shape,
My karmic actions will resonate for eternity,
Oneness with the Infinite, once I shall achieve,
And I shall continue to live as Metaphysical
Me....

Universal Query

What is life?
Is it just an epiphenomenon of mind?
That some philosophy so proudly claim,
Or is it real and earnest?
Of which grave is not the goal,
Is it that I think therefore I am,
Or things exist for real?
Can I trust my five senses,
Limited by the flow of acetylcholine?
Housed inside the corporeal frame,
Often turbocharged by the rush of adrenaline,
Or there exist some supramental entity,
To mould my perception?
Struggling at the lower plane of existence,
Will life ever attain its fuller meaning and
greatness?
Always subjected to illusions of plurality,
Will it comprehend the reality?
Or just flow in the stream of consciousness,
Within the realm of time?
Will it chance upon the oddity of serendipity,
To realise the Absolute?
Or labor to achieve the sublime,
Like the great seekers of Truth?
In this world of illusory maya,
Are Enlightenment, satori, nirvana,
And the peace that passeth understanding,

Just fantasy of human foreboding?
Or the divinity's conspiracies to descend,
Beckoning the humanity to ascend,
Above the trivialities of mundane world,
To achieve the grand oneness?
But, like agitated muddy water in a vessel,
That never reveals the true nature of serenity,
I remain perturbed, ignorant, and clueless,
Unanswered of my universal query......

Transcendence

Just feel sometimes,
I stand on the threshold of my consciousness,
About to be torn apart,
Between my lower and higher self,
I get the faint glimpses of self-realization,
But the nebulous dust of materialistic world,
Still persists to cloud my inner eyes,
The subjective reality no longer intimidates me,
For it is limited to the realm of my senses,
So why should I rejoice in the ephemeral joys,
Or cry in the fleeting sorrow?
The solitary journey that began in the physical
world,
Has its destiny in the spiritual domain,
The eternal craving of the soul to achieve,
Its oneness with the Absolute Reality,
Crossing over the vast stretches of samsara,
Playing the role in the supreme drama of Maya,
Would be satiated, once I achieve - the
Transcendence...

The Pacified Soul

Unfazed by the trivialities,
That surround his ephemeral world,
Overcoming the ocean of pluralities,
Fret with cyclic waves of death and birth,
There lives a pacified soul,
Unperturbed, untouched by worldly affairs,
Salvation, his highest goal,
For whom everything converges, nothing differs,
So gracious in defeat,
So humble in victory,
Hail the noble spirit,
Living in full glory,
Finest of minds, ever to be seen,
Outshining all that have been created,
Ensconced happily in thoughts clean,
Where the world of understanding is rested...

Why am I a Recluse?

Why am I a recluse?
To my very own emotion,
Why do I refuse?
The call of my ambition,

What has the world given me?
To make me so indebted,
When I just disagree,
With whatever I have inherited,

Life is so beautiful,
Beyond the comprehension of my mind,
And to make it meaningful,
I just follow it like the blind,

Just in a hope of knowing the purpose,
Of being here, and breathing alive,
And before the Almighty when I stand to depose,
I get entangled in this existential hive,

And I search for the reason, once more,
As to why I become a recluse,
Then I find life has opened a new door,
Where a new world is waiting with good news...

Seeker

In the solemn stillness of my reclusive silence,
I seek within me that elusive answer,
Lying on soft pillow of my sleepy conscience,
I reminisce the dreams I have woven so far,

The Ideal One

Blessed is he,
Who has serene mind,
In this world of falsity,
No results to find,

Content is he,
Who has no desire,
For it's only the evil,
That puts mind on fire,

No hope to succeed,
No fear for failure,
Happily he will ever live,
Away from world's allure,

Call this not indifference,
For it springs from ego,
But an essence of innocence,
Which inside the human bosom grow,

SCIENCE

Commemorating 50 years of Lunar Landing (20 Jul 2019)

For eons, Thou had caught the fancy,
Of the ordinary mortals here on earth,
And caused tides across the mighty seas,
And lunacy amongst us,

So beautiful, our nearest cosmic neighbour,
A silvery ball older than time,
Finally conquered by men of valour,
With one small step for man but a giant leap for
mankind,

Chandrayaan 2 - India's Tryst with Moon (06 Sep 2019)

One more day to go,
I am anxiously waiting with bated breath,
What perhaps could be the greatest show,
Highlighting the achievement of India's scientific creed,
Vikram is about to soft land on the moon,
And Pragyan to explore the uncharted terrain,
India would be amongst the elites soon,
No more land of snake charmers, but of super brain...

A Dream of a Star Trekker

If I had the speed of light,
I would embark on a space flight,
Escaping mother Earth's gravitational field,
I would venture into cosmos, deep,

I would fly past those man-made satellites,
Hanging in the sky like celestial lights,
And would follow a shooting star,
That fulfils the wishes of lovers, here,

I would rendezvous with asteroids,
Telling the fate of earth visiting meteorites,
And wait for that sluggish Halley's comet,
That appears once, when half the mortals are
dead,

Of beautiful Saturn rings, I would make rounds,
And my happiness would know no bounds,
And then follow the trail of Voyager,
In its odyssey into deep space, unfamiliar,

I would then soar into heavens,
Where I would be greeted by many suns,
I would visit the twelve zodiac constellations,
That have influenced the fate of earthlings for
generations,

On my interstellar travel,
Many myths would I unravel,
I would run to the edge of our Milky Way,
Beyond which, many unknown worlds lay,

I would sightsee the grandiose Andromeda
galaxy,
The jewel in the crown of my childhood fantasy,
As a fanatic star trekker who travelled solo,
Guided by motto "to boldly go where no man has
gone before"

Then I would make my homeward return,
To my mother Earth as a widely travelled man,
Just to find her no more in her place,
Along with other planets, vanished in space,

And I would feel the cosmic loneliness,
Realising life is a fragment of infinite
consciousness,
Burdened by hatred, ego and malice,
Leaving us, whole life, gasping for love, care and
peace...

Digital Life

Life was more beautiful and meaningful,
When the world was bulky and analogue,
When we had connections, direct and plentiful,
Instead of gossiping on a social blog,

Far more than the Moore's law could predict,
We multiplied the computing speed,
In our pursuit to outperform and exceed,
We live a digital life sans emotional need,

Once thought to be invincible,
Today, our ideas are digitally encoded,
And trapped inside a memory chip,
Left exposed brazenly in cloud storage,

No longer, we live in the world of fantasy,
That, in childhood we dreamed about,
Now we are the slaves of virtual reality,
Whose imagination runs through wired network,

Now, our virtual self is omnipresent,
Inside the world accessed by account and
password,
Like a virus, we can, as many times, mutate,
We are beyond the reach of death and birth,

One day, forever, I shall close my eyes,
But my digital life shall ever endure,
Encoded in the form of memory bytes,
As a relic of digital world, for sure,

CORONA

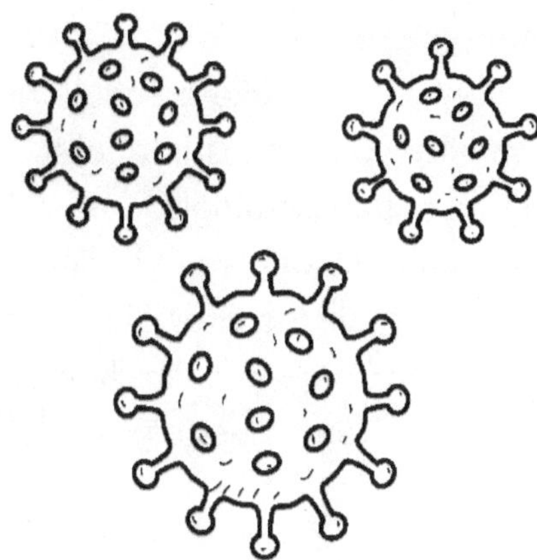

Corona-I

The Rise of the Virus

From the historic city of Wuhan to Bologna,
Has spread the tremors of deadly Corona,
That has reared its ugly head, like a hydra-
headed monster,
Spelling out recipe for a global disaster,
Prevention being the most effective solution,
When scientists are toiling hard for its vaccination,
And pharma companies are in competition,
To overcome a scourge that many regard as
biological weapon,
For a lay man, the rule is simple,
Avoid mass contact, and take precautions ample,
Wash and sanitise your hands frequently,
And put on masks unhesitatingly,
Don't spread rumours nor give in to lies,
Put up a united fight till the virus dies,
And accept the challenge to entire human race,
That seeks to kill all regardless of color of face...

Corona- II

Havoc Unleashed

Oh Corona! what have you done?
In a matter of weeks, you have left ghostly towns,
You have brought entire world to its knees,
Panic reigning everywhere, all scared of the
dreaded disease,

You have thrown life out of gear,
And suddenly we have lost our social touch,
Now we take every step in constant fear,
And swear at you sitting alone in couch,

Like death, you are a great leveler,
You discriminate not between face, skin nor
colour,
Insidiously, invisibly you tend to spread,
Feeding our mind with fear and dread,

It's amazing that a lowest life-form just a protein
molecule,
Could wreak havoc across many a nation,
Making the intelligent humans an object of
ridicule,
Surely the biggest irony of biological evolution,

Maybe it's our fault in provoking you,
For you had coexisted peacefully for years in
nature,
And it was only our fetish for bats and pangolins
for stew,
Unmindful of the pathogens hosted by the
creature,

Now we can only pray and fervently hope,
That vaccine against you is discovered soon,
Apart from quarantine, there seems no other
scope,
To escape from you, Oh deadly contagion...

Corona- III

Biological Enigma

For billions of years, natural selection has been
tweaking and tinkering us,
We've gone from amoeba to reptile to mammals
to homo sapiens,
And then suddenly comes this invisible,
contagious virus,
Posing threat to the universal evolutionary
process,
No more can we now boast of our intellectual
superiority,
That we occupy top place in the biological
hierarchy,
Now we are made to realise our innate fragility,
By the lowest life-form, that is threatening the
entire humanity,
Leaving the scientific world scampering to find the
panacea,
To deal with this modern biological enigma,

Corona - IV

The Day Our Earth Stood Still

Generations to come, shall scarcely believe this
story,
A tale of besieged times almost surreal,
A weird chapter in mankind's chequered history,
Of the events on the day our earth stood still,

No longer there's sweetness in the air we breathe,
Even in the evening breeze, there's a strange chill,
Hastily to homes we all retreat,
All on the day our earth stood still,

Clearer was the sky, purer were the springs,
Nature was cleansed, everyone could feel,
But homebound us, we missed all those beautiful
things,
All on the day our earth stood still,

Poor were the most hard hit,
Given were they the roughest deal,
Walking on empty stomach they continued to
bleed,
All on the day earth stood still,

No longer is love in the air,
To come out of home has become an ordeal,
Virus seems to be lurking everywhere,
All on the day our earth stood still,

Nature had her own way of showing anger,
That nothing happens according to human will,
Cornering humanity to the edge of danger,
All on the day our earth stood still...

Corona - V
The New Normal in Post-Corona World

Now the world ravaged by the virus,
Is slowly limping back to normalcy,
And question has already begun to arise,
Of how our new life would be,

No more can we hang out with intimacy,
Cloud of fear will always loom above us,
On constant vigil we always have to be,
Lest we be doomed by the invisible virus,

No more can we now see the crowded frenzy,
Socialisation has become custom of the past,
All protective of themselves, breaking the spirit of unity,
Individualism would now have the last laugh,

Now there would be widespread job losses,
People would struggle for existence,
They have to pass through painful phases,
All would have to practice economic penance,

Smile will be hidden, missed will be its radiance,
Fearing virus, not love, that would be in the air,
New would be the rule of alliance,
Redefining the meaning of love and care,

Sunset would lose charm of evening dine,
Uneasy social distance would spoil the party,
Stay safe at home and work online,
Would be the new norms for the entire humanity,

It would be hard to define in a word,
But surely it should be very dull,
So strange would appear our own world,
As we adapt our life to the new normal...

Corona - VI
The Second Wave

Facts are stranger than fiction, they say,
As people are left gasping for air,
Hospitals are turning into a Covid hell,
When government had known full well,
That the second wave would be more deadly,
But alas, they are late already,
And now the blame game has begun,
Between the centre and states over the supply of
oxygen,
Suddenly the leaders have realized their follies,
That they were the real Corona super spreaders,
By holding election rallies,
Even the NDMA which is in force,
Could not prevent the situation from going into
worse,
And now, we all stare bleakly,
Surrendering to the virus, meekly,
At the mayhem that it will bring,
Along with pain and untold suffering,
But still we need to brace ourselves,
Against the pandemic with our little resources,
And pray that we tide over this monstrous
problem soon,
That has left us all shattered on the path of ruin…

Author's introduction

Name: Saakal Dewan

1. Address: S/o Late Sivananda Dewan
   Village: Gelongtar
   Ging Tea Garden
   PO Lebong
   Dist: Darjeeling
   State: West Bengal
   India- 734 105
   Ph: 97758 41908
   Email: saakaldewan@rediffmail.com
2. Edu Qualification: MA (Economics), PG Diploma in Rural Development
3. Occupation: Retired Indian Navy
4. Hobby: Reading, writing ,playing chess

Presently I am engaged as a freelance writer and social activist, occasionally contributing to local dailies of Darjeeling region on issues of public interest. Most of my write ups have been published by the regional online news portals Darjeeling Chronicle and Darjeeling Times and some by the English dailies of Sikkim like Himalayan Mirror. Besides writing, I spend time in promoting sports in my region.

www.ingramcontent.com/pod-product-compliance
Lightning Source LLC
Chambersburg PA
CBHW051446130726
47987CB00005B/2204